Anxiety, Nothing to Worry About

Anxiety, Nothing to Worry About

No jargon, comfortable, easy read book for
Teenagers, Adults and Counsellors dealing
with Anxiety, Panic Attacks and Phobias.

Jeannie Philpott

authorHOUSE®

AuthorHouse™ UK Ltd.
1663 Liberty Drive
Bloomington, IN 47403 USA
www.authorhouse.co.uk
Phone: 0800.197.4150

Published by AuthorHouse 06/11/2014

ISBN: 978-1-4969-8183-7 (sc)
ISBN: 978-1-4969-8184-4 (e)

Dedicated to my little mentors:

Emily & Jacob who have inspired and tirelessly helped me craft my book in a way that is easy for teenagers as well as adults to read. Big eye popping hugs and thanks to you both.

A very special thank you to all my former clients for allowing me the privilege of understanding their own struggles with anxiety, and the pleasure of watching their recovery journey.

Massive thanks to Merryn, Barbara and Ingrid for helping me realise my little dream.

Thank you

Illustrations by: Ingrid Wheeler.
www.ingridwheeler.com

Relax you are not going crazy. Anxiety is not harmful.

It really does not matter what form of anxiety you are suffering with, this book is designed to help you.

Phobias or fear of places/things like: shops, cinemas, trains stations, being alone, crowds, family or school gatherings/meetings, college, flying, spiders, birds, people, small/big places, heights, lifts, water, snakes, fish, bees, the dark and going out are all very common. Anxiety is treatable.

This book will inform and support you as you deal with these feelings and anything you have a fear of. It will also help you deal with fear of the feeling itself.

This book will not change who you are, but it will help you find your true, calmer, happier self again.

Yes it is a permanent fix.

Understanding anxiety will allow you to see more clearly, looking at life from a positive, logical, and realistic viewpoint.

Life will feel calmer and more organised.

Working gently at your own personal pace, you will soon feel quite comfortably normal again.

I will be here every step of the way through this book.

Contents

////////////////////////////

Before we start

///

To introduce myself I am Jeannie Philpott born in 1955 and lived in the West Country all my life. I am a qualified C.P.C.A.B. Counsellor having worked with all ages and specialised with young people including those dealing with bereavement, anxiety, phobias and anger. Whilst I am now a proud Grandmother to seven grandchildren, when I was in my early 20's I too suffered from overwhelming anxiety. I discovered this method really works and surprisingly quickly. In my book I have used my personal experience and involved other therapies I found useful to support my counselling. Alongside the knowledge and understanding I have gained through my personal experience and Counselling. I have incorporated my study of art, psychology, child psychology, my personal research of nutrients, aromatherapy, colour and subliminal music to create my book. My aim was to collect my learning, research and experience together and produce a little book that would be comforting as well as easy to read and understand.

I really trust in this method and hope my knowledge and experience will be valuable to you in your recovery. I wish you a wonderful journey of discovery and healing. I honestly believe you will find considerable change whatever your age, sex, race or religion when you read this book. I hope you will feel more comfortable every day dealing with your personal anxiety now and in the future. It does not really matter how anxiety is affecting you now; this method is universal and works with the cause as well as the symptoms.

I will not be trying to impress you with my knowledge of the English vocabulary, Psychology, Counselling or the jargon that goes with it. I simply want to help you become free from the horrid feelings that may be hampering your happiness in life, at the moment and in the years to come.

I will be avoiding all references to different conditions, labels, therapies, methods and styles of Counselling, and diagnoses. I will avoid endless letters of abbreviation that can leave us bamboozled, confused and even more anxious, as we try to fit our symptoms to different phobias, obsessions and compulsions. I feel it really does not matter what we label these conditions as anxiety seems to create and heighten symptoms. So if anxiety is making you feel uncomfortable then it follows that dealing with it could make you feel better, whatever you have been diagnosed with or however your anxiety is affecting you.

Many phobias may be completely cured with gentle understanding and desensitisation to the phobia. Gradually introducing the thing you are most afraid of while using this therapy could help you conquer your fear phobia. I used to be spider phobic and after learning about anxiety gradually introduced tiny spiders onto my hand, then thought about them as afraid of me. I realised I had the power to take their life and how vulnerable they were. Now I usually help them, big or small, into a container and escort them outside to a friendly bush. I could not have done that until I learnt how anxiety works and how to deal with it in a positive way. I was really scared of flying and seemed on one long panic attack, which subsided and came flooding back throughout the journey. One day I went with a friend who had flown micro light planes and who really loved the exhilaration of lift off. She was so excited saying "here we go . . . I just love this bit it is sooo amazing, look out the windows it's so wonderful . . .", that it rubbed off on me. Before I had been afraid to look out the windows and had missed the best part of the buzz. I decided: What's the point of worrying about something when you have handed over control to the pilot. It's his problem not mine, so I can relax and forget about it.

I hope you will not only gain freedom from your anxiety but actually feel safe while you absorb information. I hope you will remain free from the fear of anxiety for the rest of your life.

First and foremost I feel it is important that you understand I have been there with anxiety and full blown panic attacks, and know just how unbearable, exhausting and downright weird it can feel. I want you to know you are no longer in there on your own with it. You have me through this book now, understanding how you feel and working with you. Use this book as a support system in any way you can and especially to help you understand the thoughts in your head. It will be ok. I know it's really unpleasant right now, but there is a way out. You have the key now and it is a permanent fix.

I will be doing my utmost to make sure you have all the resources you need for a speedy and permanent recovery. You may come up against anxiety again in the natural course of your life but it is likely to have much less impact if you know how to deal with it. You will understand how it works and be able to send it packing quite quickly.

I have put my little story in the next chapter. This may help to give you an idea of how we are all affected differently. I am not just a Counsellor but have been there too and know how horrid it is. I also know that this method works. So try and use all the parts of it when you work through the book.

Sit back and enjoy your journey of recovery at your own pace.

Life is about to get a whole lot brighter, calmer and more enjoyable.

My story

I was a young Mum about 24 years old and had my three beautiful children to look after. Two were at school and the third was due to start in six months. Money was very short, well to be honest zilch in between odd jobs. I had a heart condition which put me out of action frequently. Both were things I felt I could not control, but there was another issue I was almost ignoring and that was: What was I going to do without my youngest child with me? I enjoyed spending precious time with all my children and she was the last to go off to school. It seemed for a long while that tending children was my purpose. Now I needed to go to work to earn money which was really unknown territory for me then. All I had known for 9 years was being in the house with the children. It was approaching fast and there was nothing I could do to stop it. Suddenly I lost two close young cousins in shocking accidents followed by my Uncle. My cousins were in their late teens and early 20's. My anxiety seemed to come from nowhere. I had a bad panic attack after a very stressful evening. This was the first time anyone explained about the paper bag to help as I was Hyperventilating (over breathing). Breathing in too much oxygen in a state of panic increases the uncomfortable feelings in your body; this is quickly corrected if you breathe into a paper bag or your hands cupped together. I was referred through my doctor to a self-help group, which I found very useful and I researched anxiety through books. Life improved dramatically although circumstances did not change swiftly at home, my perspective changed. I looked at things differently and one piece of advice always stuck in my mind. If something feels really big, ask yourself: "Does it really matter? Am I going to die if I do or don't do this?" I have never come up with an answer that means I am actually going to die. In reality it would be: "This may be unpleasant for me but it is ok."

Life became brighter and less worrying the minute I understood and practiced positive thinking.

Anxiety can only feed on negative thoughts and we have the power and choice to feed our minds what we like.

The hard work came with recognising and saying "stop" to the negative thoughts and replacing them with positive thoughts and words. I made a list of positive thoughts to use during stressful times. I worked hard replacing them and felt better every day. I managed to get a job with an attractive salary. I took some evening classes and gained several qualifications. I learnt anxiety is normal and it is ok to be with it. I learnt how to bring anxiety down quickly, how to think positively, and most importantly how to make time for me and say "no" to other people sometimes. Later in life I learnt that it doesn't matter where the panic or anxiety is coming from or the reason. The method described in my book still works. I learnt just how strong this method makes you as an individual to cope with just about anything life throws at you.

Well that is my story. My point is everyone's story is different and we do not always see or understand where the stress is coming from. Really I was finding it difficult to face change, but there was a lot of stress around me. Stress affects us all individually. Understanding what led up to the anxiety can help but is not necessary for a full recovery. Writing your own story may help you to understand what you need to work on with positive thoughts as well as day to day things. Change usually has some positives as well as negatives, so try and focus on the new positive things.

We will all have more stress at some times of our lives than others. Anxiety is likely to be a result of just too much all at once.

Learning to say "No" can be hard at first.

I have a motto try anything once, within reason and if I don't enjoy or even like it or want to do it, I don't. If it is essential for my own welfare to do it, then I find ways to enjoy the activity or make the best of it. Many people don't like upsetting others but sometimes you just need to learn nice ways of saying: "no" and practice them. This is not avoidance it is choice. Avoidance is when you want to do something for instance speak to a person or go into the butchers and choose your meat but find it easier to avoid doing it. You may find the queue too hard to handle because you feel so uncomfortable with your anxiety. You may want to see your child's school play but find it too hard. Perhaps you're in the play and find it hard, or perhaps you're finding it hard to ask your boss to let you off in time to see your child's play. These are the things that are worth challenging and working on. When you are able to step through the fear barrier it is remarkable to find that people often respect you more. Remember sometimes the, 'New You' can take a little while for others to adjust to, so you may need to give them a little time to let the dust settle.

Do it if you want to and at your own pace. You no longer need to accept being pushed around. You can say "No", and you can say "Yes", it really is up to you. Take a moment to think about the difference, and also be aware that anxiety can encourage you to avoid situations that you have found stressful in the past

Little by little you will get there. Challenge your fear and feel the awesome exhilaration afterwards.

Interestingly others can develop fears and try to pass them onto you, so always ask yourself is this what I feel or is this their fears. For instance someone is afraid of spiders and says all their children are too, but often this is because the children have grown up seeing their parent act in a frightened way around spiders. Fear in many cases has to be taught. Someone who is frightened of heights may fearfully say to you: "don't go up there you may fall", when the place is quite safe to go up and you may not have been worried before.

Try not to take on other people's fears.

It is important to always ask yourself: what is stopping me doing this? If it is because of the feeling of fear then charge straight through and do it anyway. Tell yourself all the time that you are safe and doing well. You are brave and you are stronger now because anxiety no longer holds the power. You choose what you want to do and you do not let a bit of anxiety stop you anymore.

It is your life and you are enjoying it more every day.

The awareness to tell the difference between your fears and other peoples is very interesting.

Understanding anxiety cannot stop you doing what you want to do now, with respect for yourself and your wellbeing. Make informed choices about what you will and will not do now without letting the anxiety decide.

You may feel fear but now you will be able to decide rationally. Feel the fear and watch it disappear!

I do not let other people tell me what they think I should be doing, because that fulfils their needs not mine or yours, and is rarely the right choice for us.

If you are saying I should do this or that ask yourself, who is presenting this should. Is it what I want for myself? Usually it is because someone else has told you this is what you should do. Try changing the 'should' to 'could' and see how you feel. 'Could' implies a choice, and 'should' implies expectation from another. Your choice is important.

Learning to take the pressure off yourself is as important as challenging the fears you have developed in the past and are working with now.

Be kind to yourself and acknowledge your progress.

Value your achievements and try to make a little space for yourself. Perhaps make a few moments of peaceful harmony just to be at one with the world, or time to do something just for you.

Your Diary

//////////////////////////////

**Buy or make a beautiful
diary to record
your daily thoughts,
experiences and
progress but most
importantly enjoy.**

Why not make one which could be really special for
you. Perhaps cover it in fabric or special paper that
suits you, or fasten different papers together as you
write them with ribbon or string. Make it yours. It is
important that you make areas for lists, either in your
daily writings or in separate areas it is entirely up to
you. You can have more or less than the suggested lists
but these are the ones that could help you understand
quite quickly what is going on and how to change it. You
can draw, paint, write or even stick things in because it's
your diary you can do what you jolly well like. Measure
how your anxiety feels on a scale of 1-10 and chart it
daily, especially before and after events, challenges or
anything you find difficult.

**The point to remember is: It doesn't matter how
you do it but it does matter that you do it!**

Make space for lists:

List your thoughts for the day,

Your ideas (nice things you want to do),

Your daily anxiety levels, chart 1—10,

Your achievements (things you've done,)

Your challenges (things you find hard),

Your resources (things that help you),

Your positive exchanges for negative thoughts.

Write or draw anything you are feeling or want to feel, see or do in the future.

If you are female remember your hormones vary throughout the month and some people find it a little harder before their period. Be especially kind to yourself around this time and try not to put yourself under unnecessary pressure. It may be worth charting your cycle and noting your feelings during different times. If you are over 18 years B6 may help for the week before a period. Bananas contain B6 and tryptophan which could help.

If you are male and still growing remember your hormones may vary and anger and frustration are a natural part of development. Be kind to yourself and try and take time out if you feel overwhelmed by your feelings. You may want to write about this in your diary. Eating turkey breast, bananas, cheese and pumpkin seeds may help to stabilise your energy levels, which in turn may help you feel less angry. Perhaps mid-afternoon and morning try and have a snack food such as a banana or some nuts. If you feel really angry try going for a run or workout in a gym, but try and remember to eat foods with a protein in them if you can.

So if you're ready let our journey begin.

Anxiety nothing to be worried about

You really need to remember Anxiety is not harmful.

Anxiety is normal and useful in order to react quickly.

You do not need to have it switched on full all the time.

At the moment you are probably in an over anxious state a lot of the time. We need to look at quick ways to bring this into a more comfortable place while you learn how to change things quickly and permanently.

Anxiety is necessary for survival.

You are not the only one feeling this way. Just because other people look fine it doesn't mean that they are not dealing with problems and thoughts which feel out of control. If you actually told someone you felt anxious, they would probably be quite surprised that you had any problems at all.

If a fear of something feels really big introduce it gradually on a good day, with all the support you need to be able to cope. Do not push yourself to do it all at once. Go as far as you feel you want to today and take your time. There is no rush. This is your choice.

If it is not a good day you can always try a bit further the next day remembering to tell yourself all the time you are fine and doing really well.

Think about what support you need and ask for it.

No one should be forcing you.

Support is powerful, force may not be helpful.

Your Diary is very important, in it you can record anything you want to. I also want you to start making areas for lists as I mentioned before. These are very important lists of your: feelings, thoughts, experiences, how high on a score of 1-10 your anxiety feels every day, how high on a score of 1-10 the stress around you is today, your negative thoughts, your positive thoughts, your achievements even small ones, the things you found too hard today and the things that came easy. Most of all I want to know you have congratulated yourself for every single step you have managed to take toward doing things, or feeling more comfortable in situations. Make your own lists up, it can be anything you like. You are very brave to begin to look at these fears. You have courage and will become stronger every day. When you look back you will realise you are indeed a very strong person able to do anything positive you want to in your life.

Normal people get overwhelming anxiety.

We do not need to change who we are to get well.

We simply become stronger with understanding of our own power to choose our thoughts and actions.

Give yourself time to get well. There is no hurry, because if you follow the advice given in this book, every day there will be improvement and small changes until one day you realise you feel normal again. Remember there is no rush it will just happen naturally.

It doesn't really matter what kind of anxiety you are suffering with at the moment, this book will help to give you the support, information and insight you need to deal with it.

Putting yourself in stressful situations is not good for your mind or body and continued stress does affect the body and mind functions; so it can be harder to think clearly, your muscles can tighten up, sometimes causing headaches, stomach aches, chest pains and many other complaints. This does not mean you have a serious illness, but it does mean you need to look at finding a place to relax. Make time to relax and most of all learn how to relax fully. Begin to allow yourself to think about nice things, especially the things that make you feel happy and contented. Try hard to think positively about yourself. You are brave to be doing this and getting stronger every day.

While stress is not good for your body, the anxiety or panic attacks it may produce will not harm you.

Nature is just trying to take care of you by encouraging you to avoid stressful situations. Messages become confused and normal safe situations may begin to feel stressful as well. We need to inform your brain correctly that you are safe.

Anxiety comes in many forms from obsessive behaviours and thoughts, phobias of virtually anything, fears that overwhelm you, panic attacks, fear of anything which prevents you from doing everyday things and special or specific things. It may be thoughts that feel uncomfortable and intrusive so that you can't think clearly when you want to do something. Crying, anger, rituals, appetite, feeling sick, nerves, ability to function well, and memory are all affected by stress and increased anxiety. Prolonged stress can also affect physical conditions like, weight loss, weight gain, eczema, headaches, tummy problems, asthma, in fact anything that is a small problem in the body can be worsened by too much stress, so relaxation is so very important for all of us.

There are names for some of these conditions but ultimately they are all about anxiety and fear and in most cases you have taught yourself to fear the feeling of fear without realising it. Any condition which is made worse by anxiety will improve when anxiety is understood and dealt with.

Panic attacks are not dangerous.

A brown paper bag over your nose and mouth will sort out the over breathing that can happen in panic attacks. Sometimes when we panic we breathe in too much oxygen and that can make us feel worse, so a simple quick remedy is to slow down the intake of oxygen and increase carbon dioxide which we naturally breathe out. You will feel much better very quickly.

You don't need to fear the feeling of fear anymore.

Nothing is going to happen to you because you feel frightened. It will pass, like it always does.

Feeling that you are going to die is very common with anxiety, and it too will pass, so try to let go of the idea.

If you are going to die there is no point wasting your life worrying when? Life is for living and death naturally comes to us all eventually, we don't need to worry about it every day we are alive.

You may want to look at the section on: what am I feeding my mind, and body, and consider after consultation with your Doctor, taking some useful nutrients. These could quickly bring your feelings to a more comfortable and manageable level. Magnesium citrate, B6, amino acids all help. Perhaps try and reduce caffeine, alcohol, cola, sweeteners especially aspartame, salt and sugar in your diet. Pumpkin seeds are particularly good before bed to help restorative sleep, and nuts help through the day. You may find extra proteins help during the day as well. Turkey breast contains tryptophan, an amino acid that helps to increase the serotonin in the brain. Increased serotonin in the brain helps you feel calm and happy. These amino acids are easy to buy and eat in normal foods without drawing attention to yourself, and can help enormously.

Remember anxiety is not harmful to you and you no longer need to fear it.

We are going to face it together and watch it disappear.

If you feel tense breathe out all the air in your lungs, blowing out every last bit. Take in slow gentle breaths. This can really help your body relax quickly.

If you are having a full blown panic attack remember you can use a paper bag and breathe in and out while you hold it gently over your mouth and nose. This stops you taking in too much oxygen. Too much oxygen going into your system (over breathing) can encourage you to feel more anxious. It is quickly sorted out and if you have no bag just use your hands, you will feel much better quite quickly.

Distraction is also great for bringing panic under control. In a quiet, calm moment think of something you really like or something that interests you. For example: Painting, taking part in sports, sewing, craft, cooking, musical instruments, woodwork, house plans, gardening, school project, new outfit, football tactics, painting models, trains, jewellery, hair design, fashion, music you want to download, films you want to see, collecting plants, stamps, books, vintage, anything that really interests you and keeps your focus. Write your list of ideas in your diary. When you have a little time consider a project, work out how you will do it. Allow yourself to enjoy the quiet moments of planning. Save it in your mind to pick up in moments that your find your mind wandering into negative fearful thoughts. Learn to enjoy these moments of day dreaming and planning projects because they are naturally positive thinking. Get into the habit of using your quiet time usefully in this way.

Negative thoughts are no longer helpful to you.

If negative thoughts creep into your head just say "**STOP**" in your head or even out loud, it doesn't matter. You don't need to shout, to stop those thoughts. Put those thoughts away for the moment by replacing them with positive project thoughts. We will look at them together later on, after all it's not like they are going to run away if you let them go for a moment is it now?

You can safely let go of those negative frightening thoughts now.

Just try and take a few minutes each day to lie down. This can be anywhere, on the grass in the sunshine, on your bed, on the beach, on your sofa, on the floor, who cares, just anywhere you feel happy, and do some breathing exercises. Start by breathing gently in, and then breathing out long and slow, saying: "calm and relax" with each breath. Even five minutes before going to sleep at night can help mega amounts. Many people report they have a better sleep after doing relaxation breathing exercises.

Just for the next few weeks avoid stressful situations whenever you can. You could say something like: I'm sorry but you will have to excuse me I'm feeling a little anxious, tired, stressed, confused, angry, uncomfortable, sad or anything you are feeling, and I need to go away and think about why that is for me. Or excuse me I need a moment to myself. Allow yourself a moment to feel calm again.

Try to avoid thriller action horror type films and watch something a little gentler on your poor overworked brain, like a comedy, documentary, nature, period drama, learning program or film, whatever you find relaxes you, it may even be your favourite music.

If you have to wait, occupy your mind and time, really fill it up with things you have been looking for a space to think about or do.

Laughing really helps with anxiety and every time you laugh you can score yourself a big point against anxiety.

Just give yourself a little break from the hustle and bustle of life and start to enjoy your own life again.

It's a bit like stepping off the roundabout to smell the flowers, the grass, and notice the sun on your face or feel the breeze in your hair for a moment. Going fast is OK, just not all the time. Sometimes we are rushing around so much we don't get to enjoy the world around us and our own contentment and calm.

Life is made up of all these things not just stress and sometimes we just need to remember to leave a little space for our own peace, harmony and inner calm.

**Calm is a lovely feeling that is going to
take a bigger place in your life now.**

Perhaps put your phone on a quieter ring tone or even turn the sound off for your quiet time, helping you feel relaxed and in control again.

Control and anxiety are closely linked. It can feel important to be in control of your own life, but you do not need to control others unless you are directly responsible for them. Your Children and pets are your responsibility and if you are in a work position of needing to control others you may naturally be under more stress. Controlling others can be demanding. Because you may need to think quickly, naturally adrenaline and stress could be involved. Ultimately planning and training will help you in these areas. In most life situations we are all responsible for our own behaviour, our children's and our pet's behaviour. So it is worth asking yourself: Is my child over 18? Is he/she now responsible for their own behaviour? Is the person I am trying to control actually my responsibility at all? If it is not your responsibility then let it go because it is their problem how they behave not yours. A useful point to note here is we are not responsible for our parent's behaviour or our partner's.

Go and see your Doctor and explain how you are feeling. You may not want to take drugs and the Doctor will be able to support and help you in lots of other ways. It may be appropriate for you to consider the Doctors suggestions of medication. There are alternatives to sedatives which are considered non or less addictive and can be really helpful to bring your anxiety levels down. It would appear that things like Propranolol, anti-sickness, anti-histamine and antidepressants are not addictive in the same way that sedatives and opiate tablets can be, again check with your Doctor to make sure. Some people can really benefit from antidepressants if depression is an issue for them as well. It doesn't really matter how you got to feel this uncomfortable at the moment as we will look at that later. It does matter that you get the help and support you need to feel able to cope now and this is where your Doctor comes in. Also your Doctor is the gateway to counselling services which may be free to you. Counselling is very useful in looking at all sorts of issues that may have been troubling you, so please don't rule your doctor out of your recovery journey.

The last very important point to remember before you start your journey is:

Always whatever you are doing that is a challenge to you, congratulate yourself and inform your mind that you are safe while you are doing it. You are not going to die just because you have sensibly challenged one of your fears.

This is very important and your biggest skill for a quick recovery. Your mind really needs to become informed that you are safe now. If you can try really hard to do this every day things will really start to improve quite quickly. Go at your own pace with challenges but always, always, talk positively to yourself while doing them and congratulate yourself for being so brave. You are a warrior. You are winning the battle and that takes courage. Well done you for starting and brave you for keeping going. I know how hard it is, remember I've been there. This is probably one of the hardest things you have had to deal with in your life but trust me when you have learnt what anxiety is, where it comes from and how to send it away, you will be a very strong person. You will always have that strength inside you to help you through the rest of your life.

Challenging fear is not easy, but it is definitely much easier than the place you have been in, it has purpose and direction. You have a plan and know what you are doing and why you are doing it.

You will start to feel brave and courageous and know your own inner strength is powerful.

No matter what is happening remember to tell yourself every day: "I am doing really well, and nothing is going to stop me now. I have the key and anxiety will never have a hold on me again."

The world truly is my oyster now and I can do anything I want to, with respect and care for myself and others I will enjoy living my life.

What you say to yourself is very important because for a long time now you have been saying negative things to yourself, and you even allowed yourself to believe them. These thoughts are unnecessary and destructive, so say "STOP" and replace them with something positive and useful.

Don't beat yourself up if you have a bad day, we all have them, sometimes life just throws a tad too much at us in one go . . . tomorrow will be better. It's Ok.

You have control now and you can decide when you will relax and let go of your worries.

No one can make us anxious or angry, that is just how we perceive or see things and how we are used to reacting. Usually different people have a different experience when they are in the same situation because we all view things differently, depending on how we feel at the time. We may feel many emotions because of our association with past experiences or how sensitive we are. Not everyone feels or reacts in the same way.

Negative thoughts produce negative feelings which can be felt in our minds and body's.

What we feel is up to us, it really is.

Others may attempt to make us feel guilty or bad or inadequate but how we feel about our actions is actually up to us. If we know we acted with good intentions we can hand these feelings back to them.

We can learn to hand other people's unhelpful comments back to them.

You could say something as simple as "I find it really hurtful or unhelpful when you say things like that". Which makes them responsible for their hurtful or unhelpful words. Just hand it back. You may find simply handing it back helps you to feel in control of your feelings and gives you time to consider what they have said rationally. Most of all be kind to yourself; as you are doing really well, and enjoy the journey about to unfold.

What happened?

Have you ever been watching something, or reading something that really got you interested and suddenly realised you had forgotten the anxiety. However when your attention came back to yourself the feelings began to return. Didn't it feel good for the moment just before your attention came back to yourself, and the anxiety returned? Perhaps your thoughts strayed into negativity and your body began to tense up again. How lovely to have a break from it. Well you will be getting longer and longer breaks from anxiety in the future, as you practice thinking positive thoughts.

This is part of your own proof that your thoughts directly affect the sensations in your body. You have to focus on anxiety and negative thoughts for them to have any power. If you do not focus on negative thoughts or search for the feelings in your body you will not feel them. If you feed your brain positive messages through any source you will start to feel more and more comfortable every day.

Looking at how it all started for you, we need to focus on what was playing on your mind? Did something horrid happen? Did you have pressure on you for a long time? Did you suffer a physical or mental trauma? Did you have a lot of problems going on at the same time or one after another? Was someone being a bully to you at home, or work or school? Did you have more bills than you could cope with? Did you have to keep a secret? Were you struggling with work, exams, college, school or home? Did someone die? Did someone get divorced or move out of your home? Did you lose a treasured pet? Did a relationship finish? Did you move house? Did you fall out with someone, or did they do something that meant you were no longer in control of a situation? Did someone start to do things you did not agree with or put you in a difficult position? Were you simply trying to do too much? Were there more than one set of things happening during this time?

While the list is endless we also need to remember that we are all different and while someone may find a new move exciting, another person may find it hard to cope with. Not everyone likes change so several changes can be very stressful.

Life does change constantly, if we learn to expect changes it helps us to accept and deal with them when they come.

While you are trying to work out what encouraged you to feel this way, remember what is important is there will be positive change from now on. Often many things can build up and encourage us to feel anxious. It could be stress at work, a relationship, someone being ill, you being ill, or even as simple as watching a traumatic film that has set off feelings connected with something unpleasant in your life. Perhaps what you saw shocked you. Media affects us often more than we realise. Books,

T.V, films, news, web social sites, music, even adverts can have an impact on how we feel.

It is quite possible to feel anxious because you have been feeding your brain a little too much horror, thriller, murder mysteries, vampire films, wrestling, boxing, or even street/motorway crime documentaries. There is so much drama on television and in the news that it is easy to become overwhelmed and if you continue to feed your brain this information it may begin to think you are actually in danger.

It may feel like it happened overnight. Possibly, like you woke up one morning and it was just there, but we both know that wasn't really how it was. We just need to think back to what has been happening, and what we have been feeding our minds. Consider any negative information and events that may have affected you recently, from any source. Listening to music or TV can affect us and loss of anything can also have a bigger impact than you realise.

Modern film making is so realistic and even now in 3D that you can feel like you really are in danger, almost taking part in the action. Is it any wonder we have dreams and nightmares after watching something a bit scary. If you keep feeding your brain this information it can start to believe you really are in danger even though it is only a film, or TV, or a book you are reading. That is the power of storytelling we can easily imagine we are part of the story.

Perhaps you have a problem you feel you cannot work out and you find yourself thinking about it whenever you get a spare moment. You may feel anxious when you think

Jeannie Philpott

about it. Stop yourself mid thought and notice how your body feels. Are you tense? Is your heart racing? Do you feel anxious? Take a long breath out and notice the difference in your body and allow it to relax for a minute. Really concentrate on that out breath blowing every last little bit of air out, and gently breathe in again. Repeating this exercise saying "calm" with the in breath and "relax" with the out breath can really bring your thoughts and body back under your control quite quickly.

You will feel relaxed and able to function more effectively.

If you are thinking constantly about the same thing and you are feeling anxious, your mind may begin to associate your surroundings with the feelings. For example worrying about a school project or work project or falling out with a friend could play on your mind. On the way home on the bus or in your car you may start thinking about the problem and feel anxious. If you feel anxious on the bus you could begin to associate the bus with anxiety, when the bus is actually quite a safe place for you. In fact anywhere you start to worry can feel unsafe and you may start trying to avoid areas you feel unsafe in. You have allowed your mind to feel threatened by feeding it negative thoughts and fears in new situations, but these places are actually safe for you.

We are going to start to let your mind know you are safe in these situations again. You can develop phobias or fears of situations and places simply because you started thinking about your fears when you were in them. You may only have one fear or you may have many, but one by one we need to work on them and simply let your mind know you are safe in these situations. Once your mind gets the message it stops feeling fearful. Your anxiety was only trying to be useful and protect you. You need to let it know you are safe now. Inform your brain and feed it the correct, logical positive information. Remember you have fed it a huge amount of information about not feeling safe for a long time, so this will take a while. You need to repeat positive information as many times as you can, so that your healthy anxiety can protect you appropriately and keep you safe. Your negative thinking has become automatic, and you may be barely aware that you are doing it. You now need to give your brain time to accept the correct information. The more you repeat it the quicker your brain can accept it. As soon as your brain begins to accept these positive messages your body begins to feel calm and relaxed and that horrid feeling simply disappears.

Quite often when we feel things are happening that we do not agree with or have no control over we start to feel anxious, and if this goes on over a long period our minds can get a little confused about what is safe.

Well it's OK now because I am going to show you how to take a step off the anxiety roundabout.

So sit back relax and enjoy the process of learning new skills. It is your life, your body, and most importantly your mind. You have the power to do whatever you want to with all of them, it is simply about making your choices and realising what those choices mean to you.

Now at this point I can almost feel you saying: "Does she realise just how bad it is for me?" The answer is: "Yes I do, it is absolutely ghastly." I know how overpowering it can be and I know it can make you feel as if you are about to die or explode or go completely off your rocker. I understand about the mental and physical unrest you are in, and how waking can be a moment of peace followed by a surge of anxiety as you imagine the most normal things in the day being more than you can cope with. I could name so many symptoms and some people get a few and some get the full Monty. Nausea, sweating, headaches, shaking, stomach cramps, urgent need for the toilet, feeling unable to speak, feeling everyone is aware or looking at you, feeling out of place, imagining something terrible is going to happen, speech dyslexia, inability to function well, unable to think clearly, sleep problems, appetite changes and so it goes on. Some people only feel anxiety in certain situations while others seem to have it in several aspects of their lives. It can feel like the worst place in the world and you are completely on your own with it. The problem can be different for everyone.

Remember: You are not on your own with it.

Normal people get anxiety, it's OK.

Before we can go any further we need to look at Anxiety, what it is, and how it helps us function in life.

Anxiety is a good thing you do not need to fear it, but you do need to understand it in order to use it well.

In the next chapter we will look at Fred the caveman, which will hopefully give you a much clearer picture about what has been happening in your head and how you can change that.

Don't forget your Diary. It is your diary and entirely up to you what you write in there, whatever feels useful to you is just perfect!

It can be useful to write your thoughts, charts, lists and feelings in there if you want to.

You can always just use a colour for your feelings or a drawing, anything you want to do is just fine.

Fred

////////////

The Cave man. We shall call him Fred. Fred had to go and hunt for his food. Animals can be pretty fast on their feet when they sense danger just like us. So Fred needed to take things up a notch to become fast enough to catch animals for meat to survive. Fred couldn't just laze around on his stone couch and expect a deer to walk in and give himself up for lunch. There were animals Fred wanted to catch to feed his family, and animals that wanted to catch Fred to feed their families. Fred needed to learn how to react quickly to survive and avoid being killed. Fortunately we have an inbuilt mechanism that allows us to react quickly often called Fight or Flight.

Fight or flight (normal anxiety) allows our bodies to speed up and produce adrenalin which is useful for quick reactions. We can use adrenalin to fight and kill the animal for food to survive or flight to run away if it is too dangerous. Our senses are heightened, which helps us to sense danger and react quickly. Anxiety is useful.

Nowadays we rarely need to use fight or flight for killing our food or running from tigers and lions. We use it for other things, like sports, or saving a child from a busy road perhaps, catching something, using our minds quickly to work out problems. Sensing danger is still useful for survival today, but over sensing is not beneficial or helpful.

Anxiety is usually connected with survival, so money, a roof over your head, food, and warmth can be at the root of your concerns. If you do not feel safe you may feel your survival is threatened and appropriately anxiety will try and protect you. This message can easily become confused or exaggerated into: I will die without a roof over my head, which is incorrect. You will not die without a roof but it may be difficult for a while until you find somewhere suitable to live. If you are sending yourself the message I will die if I lose my job then you are informing your brain you are in danger. The reality is without a job it will be hard until you find another one, but you are not going to die if you lose your job. Tracking your thoughts in your diary will help you see if these basic survival issues are the source of your anxiety. Reminding yourself you are not going to die if these things happen will help you let go of the anxiety. Realising that we are encouraging ourselves to think negatively about a situation helps us to put things back into perspective. Life changes all the time and if you are on a low period at the moment there will probably be something rather nice just around the corner. Look at your situation again and realise there could be options. Value your options which may not be exactly what you would want, but they are usually there if you look for them. Letting go of the fear of death means you can concentrate on living and working through your current situation. If you let go of the fear anxiety follows close behind. Try and be realistic about what would actually happen if you could not pay the mortgage, if your family is splitting up, or you are afraid you will fail your exams. There will be changes but you are not going to die. Your survival is not actually threatened. Exams can always be re-sat or done with an evening class later on. Moving usually has good things like new friends and experiences. Some people say: "Oh I will just die of embarrassment if this or that happens." If they keep saying this message to themselves, the brain starts to believe they are in real danger, and embarrassment becomes a source of anxiety. It would be realistic to say: "I am uncomfortable if I get embarrassed but it's not the end of the world, I am not going to die, and it's ok to be embarrassed sometimes. Does it really matter if I get embarrassed?" Embarrassment is a normal human condition for many people. It is ok to get embarrassed.

Survival is usually the focus point if we are becoming anxious. Often we may not realise that we are worried about performing and sometimes we may be thinking if we do this or that badly we may not get good marks, or people will think badly of us. We may worry that Parents may not be pleased. We may worry about job loss, and if we lose our job or we are not clever enough to get a job how could we survive without money? It could be useful to put this energy into efforts to find a job and perhaps make or save some money by taking our junk to a car boot sale. Perhaps grow some veggies in an allotment or corner of the garden or some herbs in a window box. Worrying about the negatives does not help us live in the present and does waste our precious energy and time. Time is the stuff our lives are made of and we don't get it back so try and enjoy everything you do. Value the gift of life. Using our energy wisely is important and stress can build up if we are thinking negatively. If we do not need to run (flight) or use energy to fight for survival, we can build up adrenalin and this can make us feel quite uncomfortable.

Exercise is a quick solution to relieving stress and anxiety.

It is important to remember at this point there is an easy way to get rid of excess adrenalin and that is exercise. So if your boss, teacher, partner, children or anyone has been giving you a hard time and your adrenalin has built up here's a quick antidote: try and release some physical energy. Don't be put off if you are feeling shaky or have wobbly legs because all that will just disappear once you get going. Make an opportunity to have a quick run around the playground or your block and you will feel great when you get back, simply because you have used up the extra adrenalin. If you are stuck in an office have a mini workout, offer to make teas or sneak off to the loo and jump up and down on the spot. Just say you are exercising if anyone asks, after all it is so fashionable to be fit these days. Anything can help, dancing to a record, raising your arms up and down, just whatever feels comfortable for you. Regular exercise can help to reduce tension and anxiety in the long term as well as here and now, so it is a good idea to try and build it into your weekly routine. Walking is therapeutic and gives you chance to be away from stress and it may be worth silencing your phone and picking up messages when you get back. When you are walking you are not just exercising but you are seeing new things and refreshing your brain. Walking in the countryside or a park is really wonderful because you can stumble across all sorts of creatures, new growth and colour as well as getting a healthy supply of fresh air to help you sleep. It also seems there may be a link with sleeping well and getting outside in the daylight even for a short time during the day, so it really is a win, win situation.

Really take a moment to notice the difference in your body as you think positively.

Just step off the anxiety roundabout for a short break.

Perhaps walking the dog, cutting the grass or gardening, cycling, swimming, squash, football, bowling, cricket, garden games with the family, or even go out and boogie the night away. Aim to have fun and get exercise doing whatever feels good for you. Try and avoid alcohol and caffeine.

Fear, it's OK.

//

The feeling of anxiety when it has built up can be overwhelming and feel like your are going to die or even explode if it does not stop. Symptoms can range from one to many and everyone is different. While it is always a good idea to trot off to the Doctors and get a check-up to make sure nothing is wrong, don't be too surprised if he or she finds you fit and healthy. Often people with anxiety think they have some dreadful disease that no one has found but at the end of the day you must ask yourself the question:

How long have I had this feeling? Have I had it checked with my Doctor? Am I still alive and kicking today? Do I need to spend every day worrying about it?

If the doctor does find something wrong do I need to worry about it every day? Is it useful for me to worry?

At this point I think it could be useful to remind you again: life is in seconds, minutes, hours, days, weeks, years and we only get that second once, when the time has gone we do not get it back. We can spend, seconds, minutes, hours, days, weeks, months or even years worrying and it will not change anything at all. All worrying does is make us feel miserable and it means that we have wasted that part of our life. We do not get it back.

Thinking is useful but worrying is not helpful at all.

Most of our worries are not needed anyway and the things that are catastrophic tend to hit us blind side when we least expect them. Worrying about things before they happen is a complete waste of time. Thinking objectively about possibilities and outcomes can be useful before taking action. Worrying is simply not necessary before going to collect the children, popping to the shops, going to school or work, out for dinner or even to a party. Worrying interferes with thinking clearly about getting ready to go out. Prepare physically rather than mentally to go out when you can. If you are organised it is easier, especially with children. You don't need to imagine the whole scenario of collecting the children from school, or going to work or college. That is the stuff you just do and have the experience. However you could get your paperwork ready the night before or plan the children's or your own clothes and have them all ready, so that leaving runs smoothly.

So, my philosophy is: Yes we need to think about things to find solutions, but if those thoughts are negative or repeating all the time they are worrying. Worrying does not help anything so why waste time? Time is part of our very precious lives, when we could be enjoying those days? I say enjoy today because you do not know what tomorrow holds and you certainly do not need to worry about it.

This is your life and your choices. YOUR'S, and it belongs to you. Do not give it away to nonsense thoughts, just say "STOP" and replace the thought with a positive one.

It is your choice and simply not necessary to worry.

You do not need to fear the feeling it cannot harm you, and it will pass.

Now is a good time to make a list of positive thoughts you can replace the negative ones with. If you can't think of one ask a friend, your counsellor or perhaps have another go at thinking of one tomorrow. You didn't get like this overnight and you have the rest of your life to work on changing the messages you feed yourself, there is no rush. You may find it will just happen quite quickly as you change your thoughts. You have all the time in the world to get better. In a while you will realise the feelings are much less frequent and you don't feel so worried and anxious all the time. Remember to congratulate yourself always reminding yourself how brave you are and how far you have progressed. Every time you go out your door you are picking up the challenge of living. You are brave and will progress further each day learning to trust in the knowledge that positive thoughts feed your mind healthy information, which helps your mind and body relax appropriately.

Practice makes perfect.

Always remind yourself you are safe and feeling good about the situation you are in. No matter what you feel like, keep repeating positive messages, like:

I am enjoying this, I am feeling more relaxed every day, nothing is going to hurt me.

I am safe.

Fear of lifts, underground, tunnels, cinemas, lots of people, meetings, or fear of just talking to people can just be phobias created by negative thoughts spilling over into different areas of your life. Re-inform yourself in these situations, your brain needs feeding positive information:

I am safe. I am not in danger here. All is well.

Challenge
the fear and
watch it disappear

**Interestingly when we carry
on and do the thing that
scares us most the feelings
seem to magically disappear
and people comment they
feel great afterwards.**

So if you really can't be doing with the feeling any more just walk right through it. Anxiety has no power when it comes to physical movement. Just walk right through it. Laugh in the face of anxiety because this is perhaps the biggest key to unlocking its power! Laughter is great for making anxiety disappear.

And nothing can stop you now.

The rest of your life will be different, there could be big changes because of your new found freedom. As you progress you will find you have more power and control over your own life. This may be difficult for the people around you to accept, especially if you have been feeling dependant on them for a long time. Remember they need time to adjust to the new you. You may feel differently about situations you perhaps accepted in the past but were not happy about.

There will be positive change.

This Key of understanding has many uses, not only does it open your eyes and mind to realising just how powerful you are, you can use it anywhere. You can use it to speak, walk, run, play, laugh, cry, create and in fact do anything your heart desires that is positive and enjoyable for you.

Now it may not be easy to take the first steps but believe me it will be surprisingly easier than you thought. You will be amazed at the power you have to just step through these imaginary barriers. After all it's your imagination so you can do what you like with it. You created them and you can pull them down just as easily. You are quite capable now. The barriers are not real and you can just walk right through them, educating your brain that in reality they do not exist. You can work on the situation before you start your challenge. You can imagine the situation and remind yourself anxiety does not control you anymore. You are now stronger because you have the key and know how to wipe negative thoughts out of your mind. Remind yourself you can do anything you want now because you know you are not going to die if you do it, and you refuse to fear the feeling any longer. So what if the feeling comes? It will pass again, you are going to do it anyway just because you want to, and nothing can stop you now. Use your diary to write your positive thoughts and messages. Change your negative words.

Anger is part of fear. If you are feeling angry ask yourself what am I afraid of here? Let the fear go.

Challenge the fear and watch the anger disappear.

All anger comes from fear.

You know what you are doing and you know why you are doing it. It is not dangerous it is safe and appropriate.

Remember to write these challenges down in your diary of adventures to build on in the future. It doesn't matter if it is letting a tiny spider walk on your hand or just going a little closer to it. Just do a little more each day, always telling yourself you are safe and nothing is going to hurt you. Some people even handle big spiders and perhaps you could learn about them. Many are very safe and others may not be safe, so it's really worth informing yourself. It is a little bit like snakes, some are venomous and some are not. We do not need to fear them all. For instance some mushrooms are poisonous but some are delicious and we are not afraid of all of them just because some are not edible. Learning about our fear can also be useful to inform our brains what is safe and what is not.

Safety is important and appropriately informing yourself of dangers is also useful.

Worrying about our fears is not useful. Once you understand dangers in a situation you can act appropriately with confidence, and there is no need to worry, or experience anxiety.

Gradually build up your challenges and do not expect too much from yourself. Just do what feels good for you on that day and congratulate yourself. Some days will naturally not feel easy especially if you have been under a lot of pressure from others. Just take your time and practice on days that feel right for you.

The first time you walk through one of your imaginary barriers while reminding yourself you are doing really well, it may feel hard. Afterwards people report feeling ecstatic and really relaxed with a warm energetic buzz. It is then you realise the true power of the therapy.

Walking through imaginary barriers can give you a lovely warm buzz afterwards.

Remember little steps at first, just trying out things that are not too much of a struggle for you, and then build up to the bigger things on your good days.

Your mind can only respond to the messages you send it!

Why me?

/////////////////////////

As ironic or odd as this may seem, it may have been a choice, just not a conscious one. I will explain:

Remember Fred? Anxiety produces adrenalin which helps us to respond quickly, it is a good thing and we need it to survive.

**Anxiety is essential to our wellbeing
and we do not need to fear it.**

In fact if you think about it many people pay a lot of money to get an adrenaline buzz. They may try going on fast motorbikes, or fair rides, or bungee jumping off a bridge, parachuting out of a plane, hang gliding, or surfing the waves or anything that feels exciting and dangerous. Well that buzz can be fun and we ride it to enjoy the adrenalin rush it gives us. It is a good thing and you can ride each rush you get when you try and pick up a new challenge, as if you had chosen it instead of fearing the feeling.

You no longer need to fear the feeling.

So why are you feeling it all the time. Perhaps you may feel like saying: "I just want it to go away," "I want to feel 'normal' again." I imagine you do, and it will happen. When someone talks of normal I feel you could mean: Relaxed, not worried, not having feelings in your body of anxiety, being able to say what you really feel safely without fear, feeling confident and not that something dreadful is going to happen. Perhaps to go out without worrying about meeting someone, or be able to cope in a shop without feeling like you will shake, cry, say something silly or that people are looking at you. Being able to go out with your friends and have a laugh. Not feeling you want to cry because you are overwhelmed and worn out with trying to cope with these feelings and thoughts that ramble endlessly on. These imaginary barriers build up in our minds fuelled by negative thoughts. We imagine the worst case scenarios and outcomes of a situation.

We do not put in realistic positive outcomes as we play the imaginary situation through our minds. We just keep re running the worst possible things that could happen to us. Doing this increases the fear to a point where we may experience symptoms just thinking about what we want to do. We have continued to inform ourselves that we are not safe to do the imaginary thing. A barrier begins to form in our minds because we have incorrectly informed it. Just remember we all react and feel differently but the thoughts that create these body feelings are always negative.

**The physical feelings of anxiety are
horrid but they are not dangerous.**

After a while the thoughts may have run through our minds so quickly that we hardly notice them, but they have been there repeating again and again feeding negative, unrealistic, and often nonsense thoughts which are totally irrational and unsupported. They become internalised and we think they are real, but we have simply fed in the wrong information.

You are feeling this all the time because you are feeding it negative thoughts all the time. We are going to change these thoughts and replace them with positive logical thoughts. You will need to work hard with these positive thoughts initially but it will get easier and easier for you. You will feel more and more powerful and in control of your feelings and emotions as you progress on your recovery journey.

Rational and realistic words or thoughts are important.

Ok, now to understand how you got this way. If we remember Fred who used his anxiety adrenalin for fight or flight in order to survive, and compare that with what you have been using your adrenalin for there is a big difference.

**Too much unused adrenaline may
make you feel uncomfortable.**

Fred was using his adrenalin usefully. He used it to fight or for flight (to run away). If a wild boar scared him he could produce adrenalin and act quickly to kill the wild boar and feed his family. If he decided the animal was too big for him to tackle alone he could use his adrenalin to run very fast to escape the danger.

Adrenalin can be very useful to think quickly and move fast, it is also a good thing.

Learn to use the adrenalin wisely by exercising or inform yourself you are fine and quite safe so that it can gradually reduce.

There are two areas that will increase or decrease anxiety and adrenalin, one is what we put in our minds and the other is what we put in our bodies.

What am I feeding my mind?

/////////////////////

Probably the hardest part of your recovery is catching the negative thoughts that run through your mind, saying 'stop', and replacing them with positive ones.

Anxiety can only feed on negative thoughts.

Recognising the negative thoughts can be hard, they can be elusive and difficult to catch. Sometimes the thoughts are ridiculous or nonsense but because you are thinking negatively you accept them. Remember you have been thinking this way for a long time. I will give you examples later, but for now I think I need to point out: Counsellors can be very helpful and you could ask your Doctor if he/she would refer you to one to help you, if you wanted to. Counsellors can help you look at fears and work out with you if they are logical or real, or just something that has found its way into your mind and is complete nonsense.

Jeannie Philpott

Anxiety is an expert when it comes to feeding you an ever increasing loop of complete negative nonsense. The Counsellor may also be able to help you replace your negative thoughts with positive alternatives. You may need to be clear that you would like some help replacing the negative thoughts with positive ones.

For instance would it be logical to say:

"I will die if my teacher makes me read in front of the class",

Or: "I will not be able to breathe if I have to wait in a queue."

Or: "it will be terrible if I ask that girl for a dance and she says no".

Or: "I will be so embarrassed if I am sick when I try to walk to school to meet the children".

Or: "I will never survive if I have to give a presentation to my work colleagues or fellow students".

All of these statements are not logical or actually true and can be examined with a qualified Counsellor.

Let's tackle them now briefly:

Will you die, and I do mean actually die if you have to stand in front the class? Uhhhh Nooooooo . . .

The reality is: It may feel a little uncomfortable. You may make a mistake but all the class will be on your side because it may be their turn next and trust me they will be thinking about that not any minor mistakes you make, and you may do it brilliantly.

Does it really mater . . . No it does not.

Learn to say to yourself "does it really matter", in these situations and answer yourself with a big . . .

"Nooooooo it does not matter a jot, I am living my life not hiding in a corner and I am enjoying the experience and challenge whatever that brings."

Does standing in a queue actually stop you breathing? **Nooooooo it does not.**

Reality is: You may feel a bit uncomfortable or even quite panicky, but it will pass. Life goes on and you will cope waiting until it is your turn. You could decide to fill your head with positive thoughts. You will walk away afterward feeling you have achieved something that felt difficult for you. The anxiety will collapse when you walk through your personal negative barrier.

Every time you do this remember to remind yourself: I have done really well.

Remember to tell yourself often just how powerful you are because you physically walked through these mental barriers. The mental barriers were only imposed on you by allowing yourself to think in an illogical, unrealistic and negative way.

You are very powerful now, and negative thoughts are becoming part of your past.

Will it really be "terrible" if you ask someone something and they say no?

Nooooooo, it will be real, and ok.

If you don't ask your question you will never know.

Unknown answers can present food for a loop of questions which may roam aimlessly around your mind. This can become exhausting, going round in circles guessing at what the answer could have been and imagining negative outcomes.

It is much easier and possible to deal with realities.

"Terrible" is when a plane crashes or someone dies suddenly or there is a landslide, it is not when someone simply replies to a question. All that is important is that you ask the question so that you do not feel you have missed an opportunity to do something in your life. The answer is not important in terms of anxiety. You may feel a little disappointed but not as disappointed as you would if you had not asked and got a real answer. It is ok for people to say 'no', just as it is for you to say 'no' to something you would not like, or did not want to do.

Why will you feel embarrassed if you are sick? Being sick is no one's fault, and it is not something that is naughty, dishonest or bad. Let's look at how you would feel if you saw someone being sick. I suspect "embarrassed" would be the last thing on your mind. You would not expect him/her to feel embarrassed would you? In fact would you expect anything from him/her? I suspect you would go over and help him/her in any way you could, and if anything feel sorry for their situation. The point is, it would not be the end of the world, and you are not going to die of embarrassment if you are sick. If someone sees you they are likely to come and help and you will get home again.

Many people feel sick, or like it is hard to breathe, a bit shaky, or in need of the toilet when they are out, but the important thing is to feed your mind some positive thoughts, and to feed your body what it needs to feel comfortable. Remembering you are doing really well.

There is nothing to stop you taking a little plastic bag in your pocket if you feel sick, knowing it is there is often comfort enough to get you through. Always use a paper bag for breathing into not a plastic one. Perhaps remember a little essential oil on your hanky for a quick sniff of lavender or camomile. This feeling is not going to last forever, and as you learn new skills the anxiety and all the symptoms will gradually disappear. You are doing really well.

Sickness may respond well to gentle slow out breaths and happy thoughts. Ginger sweets, your lavender hanky and sometimes peppermint sweets may help. Finding what suits you, is important. It could be worth asking your doctor if there is anything they can give you to help if it is a particularly bad problem for you. Many anti sickness tablets can be relaxing as well, so explain to your doctor the whole problem. You need to be saying to yourself: "I am feeling great, I am no longer feeling sick, it does not really matter if I am sick. I refuse to worry about this any longer." So, pop a paper bag, and a plastic bag with a little rosemary or fresh lavender in your pocket to smell, and just forget about being sick. You have it covered if it ever happened. You no longer need to worry about it.

Feeling you cannot breathe can be helped big time with a brown paper bag over your mouth, or your own hands cupped, and let's face it they are only on the end of your arms they are readily available! If we feel we cannot breathe we are often over breathing and taking in too much oxygen and this is called hyperventilating. This is very different to asthma. Hyperventilating sometimes happens when people have been very anxious for a long time or experience a real fright. They may feel like they are not getting enough air in but actually they keep breathing in too much oxygen. This can make their arms and legs feel funny or odd. I did this once when I had been anxious for a long time and then had a really threatening situation confront me. After just a few minutes breathing into the brown paper bag replacing the balance of oxygen and carbon dioxide, I was back to normal breathing, feeling much more comfortable. After having panic attacks explained to me I tucked a brown paper bag in my pocket and never worried about my breathing again.

It is not realistic to say you will not survive because you are afraid of the embarrassment if it does not go well. You are telling your brain you are going to die if you do this thing which is nonsense, so you need to inform it appropriately and that it will be OK.

If you have to give a presentation or something similar, consider the following: Unless someone shoots you mid presentation it is highly likely you will survive to take the applause at the end!

Another little trick if you are feeling uncomfortable or not confident is to keep something in your pocket like a crystal or a stone and just feel it and focus on it. Many people say when they sting themselves or bang a toe it helps to take their mind off the anxiety, and it feels real, not like the stuff in their head. So while not a good idea to shove a hedgehog in your pocket or the odd stinging nettle, bramble or drawing pin; it could be a good idea to put something that is tactile or good to feel in there with a rough surface or squidgy ball. Those funny little squidgy creatures made of moveable soft rubber like material could be ideal. Some people feel their cross on a necklace or cufflinks or keep beads in their pocket; it doesn't really matter what it is. The focus on something tactile and real can help to take the focus off yourself and the anxiety. Focus is very powerful in distracting negative thoughts and replacing them with positive ones.

Check your diary for positive messages and ideas.

There are lots of things you can do to distract yourself from negative feelings if you are finding it hard to be positive on a particular day. Take a pleasant book with you and read it. Play a nice game on your mobile. Play positive music on your iPod. Take some crotchet or knitting. Take a magazine to flip through if you are waiting somewhere. Occupying your mind with something restful or interesting gives it a break from the worrying.

Anxiety can only feed on negative thoughts.

Distraction and positive thoughts dissolve anxiety.

Have you noticed if you are really engrossed and interested in a film that is not too full of action or thrills that briefly your anxiety will have disappeared? You may stop and think: Oh it's gone, that feeling it's gone and then because you have put all your energy into focussing on the feeling again it returns. Well it is that simple.

Anxiety cannot function without negative thoughts

You will have taken in a lot of information to use whenever you want to when you have finished reading this book. Anxiety will never control your life again. During periods of stress in your future life anxiety may build up and need attending to. The big difference is you will know how to deal with it and that is why it will never control your life again.

Just as action, horror and thriller type films may increase your anxiety levels, so too will lovely stories that capture your imagination give you a sense of peace and relaxation. The more tranquillity and peace you have in your life the quicker you will feel better. If your brain does not get much space to worry because your head is full of nice things it begins to realise anxiety is not necessary.

It really is down to you how quickly you choose to get better. You have lots of resources to use when you are finding it hard to come up with your own positive alternatives to the negative thoughts. My advice is to use as many as you can, whenever you can.

Notice how powerful media is and record how you feel after watching stressful or pleasant television.

What am I feeding my body?

If you feed your body alcohol, nicotine, caffeine, drugs or too much sugar it is likely to react to stress differently. While some drugs and alcohol can feel as if they are helping you feel calm, they may actually be increasing your anxiety and uncomfortable feelings. It is best to try and avoid them whenever you can. Make yourself aware of any medication side effects that you may be taking to discuss with your doctor.

Cannabis is not a safe drug and some people may experience paranoia, anxiety, lack of motivation, tiredness and all sorts of other mental problems after taking it.

Inform yourself about drugs.

You will find youth centres, hospitals and some doctors surgeries have plenty of leaflets you can take away and read at your leisure. Recreational drugs can be explained but never described as safe because they all have side effects, some of which can be very serious. Many recreational drugs can increase anxiety and are better avoided totally.

Alcohol can feel great but remember it is a drug and again it could calm you initially but the next day if you have too much you could feel very ill and not very relaxed or chilled at all. It's all about balance and perhaps if you are over 18 and having a couple to unwind with friends it could be relaxing now and again, while getting blotto every Friday and Saturday night, or Sunday benders, may not be such a good idea.

You can produce your own lovely buzzy feelings naturally.

Moderation is the secret. Learning to relax without any aid from alcohol, drugs or sugary foods just because you choose to is a great feeling. True relaxation will give you a different kind of natural buzzy feel good sensation.

Many people say they need their shot of caffeine to get them going; well if you are suffering with anxiety you certainly don't need a shot of anything to get you going, you are firing on all cylinders with adrenalin to spare!

Consider exchanging cola for sparkling water, and buying decaffeinated coffee. Perhaps introducing it as the day wears on toward evening, gradually getting it back to earlier in the day. There are some really good coffees out there and personally I love Cart'e Noire, which many people say is notably enjoyable and have no idea it is decaffeinated; Nescafe' also do a good one. There are also some gorgeous fresh decaffeinated coffees and coffee beans, and many coffee houses and hotels serve delicious decaffeinated coffees. You will find changing really makes a difference to your anxiety levels.

Cigarettes or tobacco again may feel as if they are calming you down but they may actually be increasing your stress levels. I know it's hard but cutting down slowly may help. Perhaps try going onto nicotine substitutes with the advice of your Doctor. Your Doctor is there to help you overcome these addictions so it is always worth going to talk to him/her. Remember tobacco and cannabis are carcinogenic and do increase your risk of cancer, so that could be one less thing to worry about.

None of us are perfect so just remember also it is one step at a time. You are doing just fine, there is no need to beat yourself up if you have weight to lose, or cigarettes or drugs to remove from your life, relationships to sort out, or moves to make. Everything will happen at its own pace and tackling one thing at a time is a good idea, for now.

The way we think is what is important now, and the realisation that we have the freedom to change anything we want to in the future to a more positive position is helpful. Making future plans is very positive.

You choose what happens now, and you can choose what you will change in the future.

Don't forget to keep writing your diary

On the plus side

//

Foods and supplements that can help to reduce anxiety are useful, but when taking supplements please check with your Doctor first. Supplements are recommended for over 18 years only and only after checking with your doctor.

Foods and supplements containing B6 can be useful if depression is affecting you. B6 helps to form Serotonin. Serotonin helps you feel calm and happy. B6 is also helpful in the conversion of an amino acid called Tryptophan that can help the production of serotonin. B6 and Tryptophan are both found in bananas.

Foods and supplements containing Tryptophan can be helpful in fuelling the production of serotonin levels in the brain which help us feel calm, sleep and feel happy. You can buy this as a supplement from a reliable source. There are high concentrations of tryptophan in pumpkin seeds, and lean turkey breast, which are very beneficial eaten before bedtime.

Consider taking a good vitamin and mineral supplement with your breakfast which can help to make sure you have the correct daily allowances. Remember a good diet with organic foods can do wonders for your body and mind. It is a shame that extensive farming seems to have literally farmed some of the minerals out of our soil and many people find they feel better when these are replaced. Organic foods can help.

One mineral I cannot promote highly enough is Magnesium Citrate and guess what, it is used up very quickly if you are experiencing a lot of anxiety. Lack of magnesium in the body increases anxiety and nervousness.

I discovered this by accident while I was searching for a natural remedy for restless legs and read several articles explaining how magnesium could help. I didn't expect much really if I am honest, but to my surprise it gave me a feeling of calm relaxation within about half an hour of taking the supplement and without any side effects. Now you cannot just take loads of it, and usually about 200mg for an adult is recommended initially to be taken about 1-2 hours before bed, gradually increasing to no more than 400mg if necessary until you have built the supplies back up in your system. Please check with your doctor first.

Freshly juiced beetroot juice which you can buy from many supermarkets now is a great energy booster before exercise and has loads of healthy nutrients. It tastes sweet and is better diluted with apple juice.

Always check instructions and ask your pharmacist or health shop advisor for advice if you are buying nutritional supplements. Always check with your Doctor before taking supplements especially if you are under 18, but you could increase foods rich in the important nutrients. It is worth checking out the list of magnesium and potassium rich foods and trying to add them into your diet.

Foods rich in iron, calcium and potassium can also help sleep if taken in the morning. Timing is very important as calcium, iron and potassium will not help you sleep if you take them in the evening like magnesium.

So if you want to feel good quickly adults could try a little B6, B complex, and a good multivitamin, if their doctor feels it is right for them. Other useful natural nutrients to try and include in your diet are: Tryptophan (an amino acid), and the minerals magnesium, potassium and calcium. Here is a list of the foods that contain significant quantities:

Pumpkin seeds, beans, nuts, avocados, spinach, cabbage, fish, potatoes, salmon, chicken, turkey, meat, banana, prunes, dried apricots, raisins, cantaloupe melon, citrus fruit, milk, yogurt, baked beans, and a little cheese.

My personal top foods for helping you feel calm quickly have to be turkey, nuts and pumpkin seeds.

Certainly high protein foods seem to help.

Smoking, alcohol and sugar could reduce the conversion of tryptophan into serotonin, so again it could be helpful to reduce these where you feel you can. I know it's hard but so is dealing with anxiety.

You are in control.

These are my personal findings and I am not an expert in the field of nutrition. What I am saying is I have discovered these things helped me and others, and it could be worth you checking them out to see if they help you. Always check with your doctor first. I can offer no responsibility for any health issues as a result of this book.

I did a lot of research before taking supplements and always checked the side effects online before trying them, to see if they suited me personally. I am suggesting you do as well. There does appear to be a lot of mounting evidence to support that good nutrition can promote a healthy mind as well as body. Additives and chemicals do seem to be having a negative effect on mental and physical health, so it does seem logical that organic healthy foods full of nutrients could help mind and body.

How much do you want to feel better?

The rate at which you get better will depend on your determination to notice when you are thinking, talking or acting negatively. That's it right there, in a nutshell, you have the bottom line!

I have worked with several clients experiencing heightened anxiety and each has reported a marked improvement after just a few weeks. Going from strength to strength they were requiring fewer visits the further they got into therapy, until they felt they no longer needed to come on a regular basis. That should always be great news for any Counsellor.

Your Counsellor is there to help you clarify the feelings you are experiencing, and perhaps some of the events or situations that led up to your present state of mind. When your Counsellor explains that positive thoughts will help you, that means you have to go away and work on it yourself; no one else can do this for you. This can be the most important and beneficial part of therapy.

Your Counsellor, Doctor, friends, and health professionals will do their best to help you, but they can only help you if you ask. Asking can be hard but saying, "I need some help with this . . ." is the first step and the rest gets easier.

The biggest problem in trying to deal with negative thoughts is recognising them as they happen, and I think this can be one of the hardest to see.

I have heard people say: "but I can't do it", and go on to explain just how ghastly the experience is, even though I may have explained that I personally have been in the situation. Sometimes they may think, 'you cannot possibly know how horrid the experience is'. Well I do, but focussing on how bad you feel does not help you get better. It can feel important for the person to let someone know just how alone and overwhelmed they feel with their thoughts. A Counsellor can be there to support you with those feelings, and help you work toward more positive thoughts. There are many different Counselling therapies and it is important that you find the right one for you. I would recommend a Person Centred approach, with a view to Cognitive Behavioural Therapy initially. You will need to ask what your Counsellor's particular form of therapy is.

If we look again at that statement: "I can't do it", and said out loud "I can do it". You would be reinforcing a positive perspective and thought process. It is that easy!

Once you start saying something positive in your head or preferably out loud you are reassuring your mind that all is well. Your mind relaxes and accepts the information.

When you mind relaxes your body follows closely behind.

You have been feeding your mind, and consequently your body, negative thoughts for so long that it is normal for you. Your mind has been told it is in danger so many times, it truly believes you are in danger. You need to inform your mind you are safe now.

The one thing you can do from now on is catch these thoughts and statements, listen to what you say. Listen to the thoughts in your head, and even if you do not feel positive you can write the negative thought down and say 'STOP' now. Use your diary and write positives to replace your negative words and statements. Pick it up and see if there is something you have already written to help you.

I can't do it.—Replace with—NEW—I can do it

There is no way I could go in there.—
NEW—I can go anywhere I want to.

I feel I can't breathe.—NEW—I have plenty
of air around me I can breathe easily now.

I'm going to be sick.—NEW—I am not going to be sick
this will pass. I have options and resources now.

I am really worried about this.—
NEW—Does this really matter?

I will die if it goes wrong—NEW—I am
fine I will not die if it goes wrong.

I should do this—NEW—I could do this it is a choice.

My heart is racing I'm going to explode—
NEW—My heart is working well this is a
healthy sign, I am ready for action.

Everyone is watching me and they know what I
am thinking—NEW—Everyone is busy with their
own life just like me and not concerned with my
thoughts. No one actually knows what anyone is
thinking they can only suppose or imagine.

I dread tomorrow—NEW—I am
looking forward to tomorrow.

Life is terrible—NEW—Life is a gift and I
will do my best to enjoy every day whatever
I am doing, I only get this day once and it
is a gift not everyone has at my age.

These thoughts are terrible—NEW—these thoughts
can be changed, it just takes a little practice

It doesn't really matter if you are still in the situation that is upsetting you or out the other side, you can change the way you think about things. Try a little at a time. Challenge yourself. "Was that a positive thought, or what was that thought?" Write it down and when you are feeling a little better or when you are with your Counsellor, or even a friend, try to think of positive thoughts you can replace it with.

For instance: "I can't go in that lift, because it could get stuck and I could be in there and not be able to breathe, no I'm not going in because lifts are dangerous." Could be: "I can go into the lift. I can tell myself I am Ok and that nothing is going to happen to me. I will be fine. I could try just one floor and practice with that first." This is a new learning process for my mind and body and I need to give it a little time to adjust to the new messages. Even in the very rare event that the lift got stuck I could breathe perfectly. There is air ventilation in the lift and someone would sort it out quite quickly. As it has not happened I do not need to worry about it, and certainly it is a waste of energy and time to worry about it every time I go in a lift. Anyway how many actual times has the lift broken down when I have been in it? Yes I am waiting, how many? So is it logical to imagine it will? Nooooooo.

There is usually a positive alternative, it sometimes takes a little longer to find it, or you may need a little help from your Counsellor.

**Don't give up on the harder ones,
just break them down a little.**

Try to remember in all these cases where things are hard for you, that you have been feeding your brain so much negative or illogical information, your poor brain believes it.

Feeding your mind negative information allows it to feel afraid, pushing it into a heightened, confused state of anxiety, because there is no actual fear to deal with. The feeling cannot harm you.

**Everything you think, say and do has an
effect on your mind and how you feel.**

If you tell yourself you can do something several times you will find you can actually do it more easily.

I am replacing my negative thoughts, words and actions with positive ones.

So you need to do this whenever you can and as often as you can. The more you do it the quicker you will feel better and understand your own power. It is the most important part of getting well.

Anxiety needs negatives to survive, you do not!

There are a lot of resources you can learn to use to make life easier for yourself. It is not easy at first but it does get much easier to recognise the thoughts. You may notice them in others when they are talking, so listen out for them every day. People say negative things all the time without even realising it. As you begin to recognise negative thoughts in yourself and others try to resist the temptation of pulling everyone else up for it! They do not have your knowledge and people do not always appreciate the advice you may be kindly offering.

If my book feels repetitive please bear with it, everything is in here for a reason. Anxiety may prevent you accepting a positive message explained one way, but may be able to accept a similar positive message explained another way.

The more you read, the more positive messages eventually become accepted. Your brain will not be able to discard the logical positive messages so easily once it understands you are safe. Once your brain has accepted and understood the logic and reality of positive thinking, you are informed. Once you are informed and understand you cannot go back to the illogical nonsense negative thinking.

Your future will always hold this key of understanding.

Anxiety will hold no power over you in the future. You cannot go back the state of mind you were in before you knew how to zap it.

Distraction and feeling happy

///

Music to calm you and subliminal messages.

Subliminal = messages you may not be aware of.

Start to make a collection of music that has positive lyrics or words in it. Listen carefully to what the artist is saying. What is the message? If it is positive make a note of it for your personal compilation CD or iPod playlist.

I will give you a list of my personal favourites, some old, some new, but they all have a very positive subliminal or underlying message. Your personal compilation of music can be played any or all the time. Play them when you are having a low day and positive thoughts seem far away. Just let the music do the work for you today.

I use music to help calm and promote positive thought. Subliminal music is very powerful. If you remember the "Children" record that was used to calm people at the end of the night clubs written by Robert Miles, you will understand the power music has to send your thoughts in any direction to change your mood and ideas.

Remember music is powerful and can encourage you to feel sad, happy, angry, calm, and many other moods.

It could be really helpful to start making your own personal compilation when you get some free time.

Everyone's taste and association with music is different so pick the ones you enjoy, and be careful to check the lyrics are all positive to help you personally.

Once you have chosen your special, uplifting, feel good songs and made your little compilation you can't play it too much. You will be amazed at the impact on your mood, thoughts and actions. Even if you are in a full blown panic attack the lyrics get through. Check it out, it's amazing.

I recommend singing along at the top of your voice proving to the anxiety and negative feelings you're the boss. You can do what you like in spite of anxiety feelings. Guess what? Surprise, surprise, the feelings start to disappear because you are feeding your brain positive messages; and let's face it, it beats sitting there thinking how bad you feel. You have been doing that for a long time now, so it's time to take control and try something positive and enjoyable. Nothing is going to happen to you if you sing while you are having a panic attack. You will feel better and you can do it anytime with your own special songs full of positive lyrics!

Feel good with your own positive music vibes.

The more you play your songs the more they get into your head and play themselves, so you will find it easier and easier to sing positive lyrics. For instance it is hard to ignore these lyrics once they get inside your head, they tend to replay naturally all on their own.

"Love lift me up where I belong . . ." by Joe Cocker.

"Pack up" . . . Eliza Doolittle.

"I'm on top of the world . . ." by the Carpenters.

"I feel good . . ." by James Brown.

You can choose the latest, noisiest, softest, or oldest that suit you best. Positive music makes the process of getting better happen sooner with more ease and less struggle to think of positive things. It doesn't mean you can stop working on positive thought replacement but it does give you quite a nice little break and backs up your support and re-education of your brain. You really can stop worrying now.

Worrying is not useful to you in any respect and the calmer your brain feels, the clearer you will be able to think and enjoy your life.

You need to find your own special songs but just to get you started here are some of my favourites, from all different genres and generations are:

AMAZING: INNA

DON'T STOP BELIEVING: GLEE CLUB

DON'T STOP BELIEVING: JOURNEY

FEELIN' FINE: ULTRABEAT. THE ALBUM 2007

FEELING GOOD: NINA SIMONE

FLY ON THE WINGS OF LOVE: DJ CHUCKY

GOOD FEELING: FLO RIDA

HEAVEN IS A PLACE ON EARTH: BELINDA CARLISLE

HO HEY: LUMINEERS

I CAUGHT THE SUN: STORNAWAY (MY FEEL GOOD BEST)

I FEEL GOOD: JAMES BROWN

I GET KNOCKED DOWN : TUBTHUMPING

I LIKE THE WAY YOU MOVE: BACKSTAGE

I'M INTO SOMETHING GOOD: HERMAN & THE HERMITS

I'M ON TOP OF THE WORLD: CARPENTERS

IN THE ARMS OF AN ANGEL: CELTIC ANGELS

JUST THE WAY YOU ARE: HIT MASTERS

LET THE MUSIC LIFT YOU UP: LOVELAND

LIVING FOR TODAY: THUNDER

LOVE IS ALL AROUND US: BEE GEES

NO WORRIES: SIMON WEBBER

NOT GIVING IN: RUDIMENTAL

PACK UP: ELIZA DOOLITTLE

PALOMA BLANCA: HOLIDAY SUNSHINE

PEACEFUL EASY FEELING: EAGLES

POWDER YOUR FACE WITH SUNSHINE: EVELYN KNIGHT

PUT YOUR RECORDS ON: CORINE BALLY RAE

RAINCLOUD: LIGHTHOUSE FAMILY

RELAX: FRANKIE GOES TO HOLLYWOOD

SONGBIRD: EVA CASSIDY

SONGBIRD: OASIS

SUNRISE: NORAH JONES

SUNSCREEN: BAZ LURMAN

SUNSHINE ON MY SHOULDERS: JOHN DENVER

TAKE IT EASY: EAGLES

TAKE ME TO THE CLOUDS ABOVE: U2 & LMC

THREE LITTLE BIRDS: BOB MARLEY

TITANIUM: DAVID GUETTA & SIA

U SEXY THING: HOT CHOCOLATE

UP WHERE WE BELONG: JOE COCKER

WALK TALL: VAL DOONICAN

WALKING ON SUNSHINE: KATRINA & THE WAVES

WHAT DOESN'T KILL YOU (STRONGER): KELLY CLARKSON

WORLD HOLD ON: BOB SINCLAIR

YOU ARE NOT ALONE: EAGLES

YOU'RE A SUPERSTAR: LOVE INC

Music and lyrics are very individual and you will need to personally choose your music. Just pick the ones that appeal to you from the list, then search around for some of your own favourites. Make sure to check the lyrics are positive and uplifting. Some love songs may make us feel quite sad and thoughtful, especially if we do not have someone special in our life. While happy cheery positive lyrics really uplift our spirits and give us a new energy to feel we are more alive.

It is essential that you tailor your music to your specific needs. We all associate different things with calm and happiness, some of the lyrics or the genre of music may not be to your taste. If you go online to iTunes or a similar music site and pop in the titles you will be able to have a listen to see if you enjoy any on the list. You need to be careful about playing music with negative lyrics for a while until your brain has been re-educated with positive messages. You may like some songs because of the voice or music. When you listen carefully to the lyrics you could begin to realise they are negative, save those for your stronger times. If you really like a less positive song when you are feeling better please try and make sure you have plenty of positive music and lyrics around them. Shops try and encourage us to buy with music, colour and even smell, some dentists play calming music, often hypnotherapy can be accompanied by relaxing music. It has become clear that lyrics and music affect people. You can use this to your advantage now.

So have a really careful listen to the words in the music you have been playing recently, and choose wisely, for your personal benefit.

Keep writing your diary it is a very powerful project.

Words and music are very powerful, and many may underestimate the effect of listening, remember if opera can make people cry, and beat can make people want to dance and jump around, it is powerful. If film makers use music to make a film feel more dramatic, sad, happy, serious or funny then your emotions are involved before you even hear a negative or positive word.

Music and lyrics (or words) are very powerful.

Choose your music and really enjoy every minute of the day. Even washing dishes or your car or cleaning your bedroom can become fun. When you are getting ready for something that you feel excited about or a little nervous put your music on to choose what mood you will be in.

**Positive music, thoughts and projects
bring positive change.**

Feeling Happy

////////////////////////////////

Make time to spend in a place you enjoy, perhaps with good friends or family, and the rest of the time make the best of whatever comes your way. Sometimes the biggest gifts in life come when you are not in your favourite place and not in your favourite company. Often when things seem at their very lowest someone can show us a kindness, a little care or understanding that can help us to feel better. These are the true treasures in life. Never feel that time spent in a hard place or difficult situation is wasted there is always something to learn from it.

There is a saying that goes a little like this: "Man or woman can make hell of heaven or heaven of hell", and we all have a choice in how we see things. We can look at life as a gift or a sentence. All that really matters is what goes on in our heads. If we are miserable it is hard for us to enjoy anything and if we are happy very little seems to upset us. For example:

A poor man in prison could feel happy because he reads books about a beautiful life and imagines himself to be part of that world. He may use his time wisely and educate himself. He may learn about others and make himself ready for a new career and life when he leaves prison. He still has options. He can try and make amends for the damage he has caused and make plans toward that, or make plans to help others in the world in some way. Perhaps his time on education now could help him to help others. He could feel happy with his efforts to change his future into a positive one. It is his thoughts not his environment or circumstances that make him feel happy and worthwhile. He enjoys his day and plans his future life. Although he is confined by prison he is living.

A wealthy man who walks in a beautiful spring landscape with the warm sun on his face can feel desolate, lonely, and anxious because his thoughts are negative. It is hard for him to feel happy or calm or enjoy the beautiful things around him. The warm sunshine and gentle breeze do not please him. He is unable to value the sounds of the stream or the brightly coloured dragon flies. Not even the natural colours of the fields lift his spirit. Just because his thoughts make everything seem pointless and he is unhappy. He imagines he is in danger constantly because he is feeding himself negative thoughts. It is his thoughts alone spoiling his day and his future life, not his surroundings and circumstances. He may be walking freely but he is confined by his mind, and has made his own prison.

We have already established: You only come this way once and every minute is precious, you don't get a replay. If only, wouldn't it be great to go back and put right all our mistakes. That is life, a learning process and that's OK. We all make mistakes, many of us get into situations we regret later, many of us do things we wish we had not. Sometimes we wish we had said or done things that we did not. Ultimately the future is ours and without letting fear chose our direction we can lead fuller more comfortable lives. We can be safe in the knowledge we have the courage to say I'm sorry, or no that is not something I want to do. Anxiety no longer chooses how you behave, but you can choose freely knowing any uncomfortable feeling will quickly pass and have no power over you.

You are in control now.

So how is your diary coming along?

What are you learning about yourself?

Daily entries are really important.

Have you achieved anything this month that was hard recently?

Have you listed the things you want to do?

Make a new list of the things you have done and how hard or easy they were to do, and congratulate yourself.

List the fears that feel a little less scary.

Have you made a list of alternative things to think about when negative thoughts overwhelm you?

Can you add to your list of positive things to think about when you feel anxious?

Anxiety is no different to any other problem you are trying to solve, you just do a little at a time.

Make lists you can refer to at any time, the better the lists the more effectively they work.

**Most importantly don't forget to write
your success stories in, even if it is
something small, it is very valuable.**

Start looking at colours and how they encourage you to feel happy, sad, excited, calm etc. There are some ideas that red encourages excitement and can feel dangerous, green encourages change and is calming, pale blues are restful and calming, yellows can be uplifting and cheery, oranges can help you feel happy or lively, purple can feel calming perhaps helping psychic ability and aid creativity, black can be heavy, and white is light and cleansing. Use them to help the way you want to feel, remembering it is how they affect you personally that matters. So wear or decorate with colours that make you feel good.

My final offering

//

Well it really doesn't matter what your negative thoughts are, as long as you work really hard on replacing them with positive ones every day and as often as you can. The more you do it the quicker you feel better.

**The Key is understanding that anxiety is
only able to feed on negative thoughts.**

If you think about it even the danger of fire has to be taught to us as small children. It is about re-training your mind that situations are safe so that you feel comfortable when you are in them. It does take a little time for your brain to really get the message, but just like the negative thoughts they build up and the new positive messages will become quite strong. Very soon all this anxiety will feel like a million years ago.

Just feel the fear and do it for the buzz stepping right through the imaginary boundary you created with negative thoughts. You will be amazed just how powerful this is in convincing your mind it is quite safe. Don't forget to tell yourself how well you are doing all the time, and that everything is fine. The mind needs good positive messages while you are doing things, and will respond better in the same situation next time. Each time your brain learns a little more that you are safe, you will feel better in the situation, until it no longer bothers you at all.

**Exercising to burn excess adrenalin is
wonderful and really helps reduce stress.**

Exercise is really important to release any extra adrenalin that has built up because negative thoughts or stressful situations have taken over. Exercise is also useful to keep your body balanced and your mind happy on a regular basis, so try to incorporate as much as you can into your daily routine. Even a 10 minute walk in the fresh air, a run around the playground or boogie with your mates can really make a big difference to how you feel mentally and physically.

Feed yourself good nutrition to help you feel calm like pumpkin seeds, nuts, turkey breast, poultry, meat, milk, yogurt and greens. Be careful with chocolate, sweets, pastries and cakes avoiding them if possible. Adults check with your Doctor first and perhaps you could get some good supplements of magnesium, tryptophan, B6 and a good multivitamin. There is a good Seven Seas Cod Liver Oil with multivitamin capsule that I like. Teenagers could ask your Doctor but it may be safer just to eat the foods that have been suggested to get extra nutrients.

Avoid caffeine, cola, drugs, too much alcohol or sugar which increase anxiety. Milk, decaffeinated drinks, natural or flavoured waters, and natural juices are alternatives that may be helpful for the moment.

**Knowledge and skills once learnt cannot be taken
away from you and are yours to use for life.**

Try to utilise and value: Self-help groups, Friends, Parents, Teachers, Doctors and Counsellors. Your own growing strengths will always be the most valuable resource in your life. You will begin to understand the power you have to direct your feelings and do the things you want to. Other people are also there to help and support you, and it is worth thinking about explaining to people you trust, what you are going through. They don't know and can't support you if you don't tell them how you feel. They are out there with a wealth of individual skills and support to offer you if you let them know you want their help. There is something very valuable in feeling normal when your problem is taken out and shared: it seems to lose its power over you and often affects you less.

Appreciate and value your friends and family.

I feel there is something very relaxing about painting with a paint brush, imagining how your finished project will look with its new fresh colour, or explore painting a picture using any medium you like. Art is very useful in therapy for several reasons. First and foremost it accesses the creative free side of the brain where all sorts of feelings can come out. Secondly you can put anything you jolly well want to in your painting; it is yours, no one else's but yours alone. There is no right or wrong, or good or bad. Your art is purely yours and valuable in its own right as an art form. Do not allow anyone to tell you any different. If you want to stick bits of paper or fabric in it, or use several different paints or even use your hands or a palette knife that is your choice. You can make it abstract or representational. It could be black and white or just one line it is up to you. Perhaps paint your room, house, anything or paint a picture and enjoy knowing only you can create this.

Relaxation is very important and I am not just talking about painting, meditation or sitting in the armchair watching TV. You can relax and be active as well, it is all about balance. Gardening, walking, photography, craft projects, writing, creative ideas and many more things can be very relaxing without trying too hard. Meditation for ten minutes can be more restful than sleep and learning the art is very simple and rewarding.

In its simplest form it is about allowing your mind to relax and consequently your body. I find counting one, two in your head with every in breath being one and called "calm", and every out breath being two and called "relax". You need to concentrate on making your out breath longer and longer literally blowing all the air out of your lungs slowly and evenly. Releasing air from the body helps it relax very quickly. Your in breaths will get gentler and easier each time and because you have to concentrate quite heavily initially to do this it can help you to ignore any negative thoughts. Quite often negative thoughts will try and push in but you have the ability to say "no" and quickly re focus on your meditation plan. Start to feel your muscles relax from your head all the way down through your jaw and shoulders in particular. Sometimes if you tense and relax these muscles it will help you to feel the difference. If you have been very tense for a long time it is hard to realise your body is not relaxed. Work your way down through your body tensing and relaxing until you get to your toes and simply concentrate on counting: One "Calm" and two "relax", with lovely long out breaths. Once you have got used to doing this you will find it heavenly and your own special 10 minutes. Remember even 10 minutes before sleep at night can make a big difference to the quality of your sleep.

Aromatherapy is very useful and some of the best essential oils to aid relaxation are said to be lavender, camomile, pure rose, neroli (good for depression as well), benzoin, bergamot, frankincense, geranium, hyssop, jasmine, melissa, patchouli, sandalwood, verbena and ylang-ylang.

YOU SHOULD NEVER USE AROMATHERAPY DURING THE FIRST THREE MONTHS OF PREGNANCY. ALL OILS MUST BE DILUTED WITH ALMOND OIL OR USED ONLY AS AN INHALENT, POSSIBILY ON A TISSUE A FEW FEET AWAY FROM WHERE YOU ARE RESTING. CHECK WITH YOUR DOCTOR AND AROMATHERAPIST FIRST. GENERALLY LAVENDER, CHAMOMILE AND ROSE ARE THOUGHT TO BE SAFER. IF YOU ARE NOT SURE DO NOT USE.

Massage can be really helpful for relaxation and this can often be combined with aromatherapy, so worth investigating in your area. Head, body, and back massage are all useful to relaxation.

Walks are wonderful for clearing your head and getting rid of excess adrenaline, toning muscles and lowering stress. Getting sunshine and beneficial light may help you sleep. Never underestimate the value of a walk in the fresh air, and fit them in whenever you can.

If you choose to listen to radio, TV, iPod or input any external message try and make sure it is a positive one.

We have looked at making music and choosing carefully what kind of films or TV you watch. As you feel better you may want to introduce the horrors of the 9pm News or a thriller film. Just be aware overload of too much stress albeit actually happening to you or someone else, does affect you and could increase your anxiety. Take good care of yourself, remaining aware of influences around you, and congratulate yourself for coping so well. Most of all remember, when a negative thought comes into your head say **STOP!** Refer to you diary and replace it with a positive one. Soon you will have learnt your positive messages and be able to do it automatically.

You will start to feel calmer and stronger everyday.

Remember it is what you do that is important. Do not let anxiety stop you doing what you really want to do. No matter how you feel keep going reminding yourself you are safe and doing very well. Have pride in yourself achieving a little more each day.

So my courageous brave warrior off you go, out into the world to strut your stuff, try out your new found resources, and do what you want to do. Enjoy yourself and do your best to make the world a nicer place as you move on your journey through life. Yours! Each day is precious so do your best to enjoy it whenever you can.

If agro comes your way remember all anger comes from fear, ask yourself what has happened or what have I done or said to frighten this person and how can I put them at ease.

When the going gets tough, remember that anxiety can only feed on negative thoughts, remove and replace them and anxiety with all its symptoms collapses.

You don't need to feel confident
to say "I am confident".

Your brain will absorb the information just the same, and the more you say it the quicker it will happen.

You have many resources to use in this book. You are back in control and you decide how and when you use your resources. Remember you are not alone, there are so many people out there suffering with anxiety who do not have the knowledge that you do. People with anxiety do not go around with a label saying I am anxious, or I feel like I am about to panic, they just quietly go about their normal day struggling with negative thoughts. Be aware of others needs as well as your own, if they look slightly uncomfortable try and make life easier for them without drawing attention to the situation.

Many books focus on anxiety and all the words that describe its negative manifestations, they categorise and explain different conditions and therapies, using abbreviations and words that are hard to understand. I have tried really hard to resist, in order to make this book comfortable, readable and easy to understand. I want to give you information that puts you back in control of your thoughts and life, so that you know how to deal with anxiety now and in the future. I feel to bombard you with a lot of frightening language and possible condition boxes you may or may not fit into, is in itself negative and not necessary for recovery.

Because you are informed you will never feel overwhelmed and unable to cope with your anxiety again. Anxiety is a positive and useful thing, we need it for survival. It is simply about deciding if we have been overloaded and need to balance things out again with some positive replacements, and a little more relaxation.

Be aware life does throw some horrid stuff now and again, it won't last forever remembering our positive thoughts help us have a much smoother ride through it.

Lastly be kind to yourself, do not expect too much on a harder day and enjoy the good ones.

To all the brave souls who are embarking on this difficult but exciting road to recovery, my sincerest thoughts and heartfelt support are with you on your journey. I wish you a wonderful life in which you are able to enjoy something every day.

Disclaimer

I am a qualified C.P.C.A.B. Counsellor but I am not an expert nutritionist, colour therapist or an aroma therapist. The information I have provided in this book is from my personal research and experiences which I have compiled together to make your own research in these areas easier. Always check with your Doctor or expert before considering a change in your nutritional supplements, or commencing a new therapy.

GLOSSARY: In the context of this book

C.P.C.A.B. - Counselling and Psychotherapy Central Awarding Body. My name was formerly Jeannie Harris.

Bereavement. - Losing someone you value.

You may also feel bereaved if you lose a relationship, or job or something you value highly.

Jargon - Special technical words associated with a subject.

Empowerment - Enable or help someone to be or do what they would like to.

Manifestations - Things that appear or show. For instance in psychology behaviours, thoughts, feelings.

Categorise - Group together and name or label.

Lyrics - words in songs.

Perspectives - The way we see things.

Resources - Things to help support you.

Antidote - Reverse the situation or feeling in this case.

Scenario - A sequence of events, or how things happened.

23506523R00064

Made in the USA
Columbia, SC
09 August 2018